Sabina

Lions

Life in the Pride

by Adele D. Richardson

Consultants:
Tammy Quist and Gena St. John
President and Vice President
Society for Wild Cat Education

Bridgestone Books
an imprint of Capstone Press
Mankato, Minnesota

Bridgestone Books are published by Capstone Press
151 Good Counsel Drive, P.O. Box 669, Mankato, Minnesota 56002
http://www.capstone-press.com

Library of Congress Cataloging-in-Publication Data
Richardson, Adele, 1966–
    Lions: life in the pride/by Adele D. Richardson.
    p. cm.—(The wild world of animals)
    Includes bibliographical references (p. 24) and index.
    ISBN 0-7368-0964-3
    1. Lions—Juvenile literature. [1. Lions.] I. Title. II. Series.
QL737.C23 R525 2002
599.757—dc21   00-012544

Summary: An introduction to lions describing their physical characteristics, habitat, young,
    food, predators, and relationship to people.

Editorial Credits
Erika Mikkelson, editor; Karen Risch, product planning editor; Linda Clavel, designer and
    illustrator; Heidi Schoof, photo researcher

Photo Credits
Craig Brandt, 20
Joe McDonald/TOM STACK & ASSOCIATES, 10
Joe McDonald, 4
Lisa & Mike Husar/Team Husar, 12
Michael Turco, 8
PhotoDisc, Inc., 1
Richard Demler, 16
Robin Brandt, 14
Root Resources, 18
William Bernard, cover, 6

1 2 3 4 5 6 07 06 05 04 03 02

10961

Table of Contents

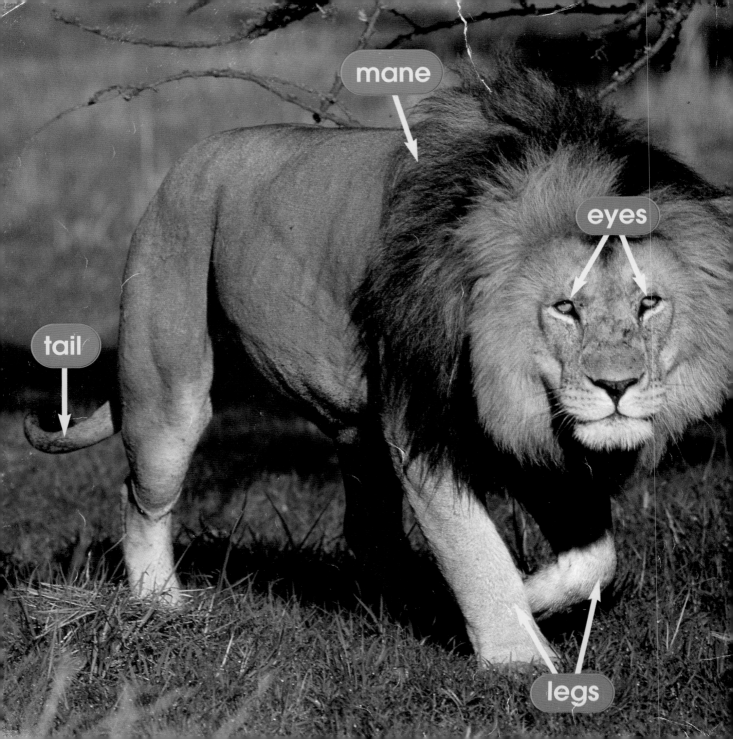

Lions

Lions are large, wild cats. They have four legs and a long tail. Lions have sharp teeth and claws. Male lions have a mane of long, thick hair on their head and neck. A lioness does not have a mane.

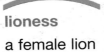

lioness
a female lion

Lions Are Mammals

Lions are mammals. Mammals are warm-blooded animals with a backbone. Mammals are covered with hair or fur. Lions have yellow-brown fur. A lion's fur coat protects it from cold weather and rain.

warm-blooded
having a body temperature
that stays the same

A Lion's Habitat

Most lions live in Africa. A few lions live in Asia. A lion's habitat is in large, open areas called savannas. Lions hunt easily on savannas. Their fur matches the color of the grass. Lions can sneak up on animals and kill them.

habitat
the place where
an animal lives

FUN FACTS ! Lions do not have back teeth for chewing. They tear food with their front teeth and swallow it in chunks.

What Do Lions Eat?

Lions are carnivores. They eat other animals for food. Lions eat antelope, warthogs, and zebras. Lionesses do most of the hunting. They quietly sneak up on their prey. They then attack the animal with their sharp teeth and claws.

prey
an animal hunted for food by another animal

Life in the Pride

Male and female lions live together in a pride. A male and female lion leave the pride to mate. They join the pride again after they mate. Two to four young lions are born four months later. Lions can mate at anytime during the year.

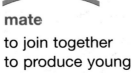

mate
to join together
to produce young

Lion Cubs

Young lions are cubs. They weigh about 3 pounds (1.4 kilograms) at birth. Lion cubs cannot walk or see for about 10 days. They drink milk from their mothers for about six weeks. Lionesses then begin to teach the cubs how to hunt.

A Lion's Mane

Lions are the only cats with a mane. A mane helps male lions look big and strong. A lion's mane is not fully grown until the lion is 5 years old. The mane becomes darker as the lion grows older.

A pride has its own territory. Male lions protect the territory. A lion marks its territory with scents. These scents warn other lions and animals to stay away.

Predators

Lions have few predators. Hyenas sometimes try to attack lion cubs. Male lions growl and roar to scare the hyenas away. Lions also fight animals to protect their territories. Lions will not allow lions from other prides onto their territory.

predator
an animal that hunts and kills other animals

Lions and People

People create reserves to help lions. Lions are protected from hunters on these lands. Many people also visit reserves to study lions. They then teach other people about lions and how they live.

Hands On: Find Your Territory

Lions mark their territory in many ways. Lions can scratch, rub, or urinate on the trees or bushes in their territory. The scent they leave behind warns other lions to stay away.

What You Need

An adult
Four or more scented objects such as an orange, lemon,
  onion, car air freshener, popped popcorn
A sharp knife
Four friends
Small paper sacks

What You Do

1. Have an adult cut the orange, lemon, and onion into halves.
2. One player should choose an object's scent to remember. This scent will identify his or her territory. This player should leave the room.
3. The other players place each object into its own paper sack.
4. The player returns to the room.
5. The other players hold each sack.
6. The player tries to find his or her territory by smell. The player cannot look inside the sacks.
7. Have another player choose a scent. Have this player leave the room and try it again.

Words to Know

carnivore (KAR-nuh-vor)—an animal that eats only meat

mammal (MAM-uhl)—a warm-blooded animal that has a backbone; female mammals feed milk to their young.

mate (MATE)—to join together to produce young; male and female lions mate to produce lion cubs.

pride (PRYD)—a group of lions that live together

reserve (ri-ZURV)—a protected area where animals have space to live and food to eat

savanna (suh-VAN-uh)—flat, grassy land with few or no trees

territory (TER-uh-tor-ee)—an area of land animals claim as their own to live in

Read More

Darling, Kathy. *Lions.* Carolrhoda Nature Watch Book. Minneapolis: Carolrhoda Books, 2000.

Holmes, Kevin J. *Lions.* Animals. Mankato, Minn.: Bridgestone Books, 1999.

Johnston, Marianne. *Big Cats Past and Present.* Prehistoric Animals and Their Modern-Day Relatives. New York: PowerKids Press, 2000.

Internet Sites

African Savannah: African Lion
http://www.oaklandzoo.org/atoz/azlion.html
The CATalog
http://www.wildcateducation.org/catalog/catalog.html

Index